Now I can . . .

Spell

Green Book

By Ronald Ridout

Illustrated by Colin Caket

Collins

in association with

 Belitha Press

Dear Adult,

May I tell you briefly what the essence of NOW I CAN SPELL is?

First, it consists of eight graded write-in books to help young beginners over the first steps of learning to spell.

The first book (Pink) begins with words of one syllable, but always with their meaning made clear by pictures. By the last book (Brown), children are spelling words of two syllables.

Children will neither make much progress, nor have the encouragement to go on trying, unless they can do the spelling. NOW I CAN SPELL is, therefore, completely self-guided throughout. The children are enabled to do the spelling on their own, and very largely without mistakes, because the means to come to the right answer is always available.

NOW I CAN SPELL is specially suited to young children working at home, as it is the most gradual and the most helpful learning-to-spell series there has ever been.

I am sure with this book and your help your child will make the maximum progress in learning to spell.

Yours sincerely,

Ronald Ridout

First published 1985 by Collins Educational, London and Glasgow
in association with Belitha Press Limited,
31 Newington Green, London N16 9PU
Reprinted 1986   Revised edition published by William Collins Sons and Co Ltd 1987   10 9 8 7 6 5 4
Text and illustrations in this format copyright © Belitha Press 1985
Text copyright © Ronald Ridout 1985
Illustrations copyright © the estate of Colin Caket 1985
ISBN 0 00 197432 7
Typesetting Chambers Wallace, London
Printed by Purnell Book Production Limited Paulton, England

Can you put the right names under the pictures?
Choose from the list below.

Like this:

crown

_____   _____   _____   crown

_____   _____   _____   _____

_____   _____   _____   _____

crab   shirt   train
shark   sweets   goal
boat   owl   crown
moon   stars   horse
darts   snail

_____   _____

feet
foot
beet
boot

_ _ _ _ _ _ _ _ _ _ _ _ _ _ _ _ _

weed
wood
deer
door

_ _ _ _ _ _ _ _ _ _ _ _ _ _ _ _ _

geese
goose
peel
pool

_ _ _ _ _ _ _ _ _ _ _ _ _ _ _ _ _

teeth
tooth
sheet
shoot

_ _ _ _ _ _ _ _ _ _ _ _ _ _ _ _ _

reef
roof
creek
crook

_ _ _ _ _ _ _ _ _ _ _ _ _ _ _ _ _

A Write the complete words, like this:

k e y ies		t e go ve	
storm	Storm	card	_____
stor-	stork	car-	_____
stor-	_____	car-	_____
stor-	_____	car--	_____
stor---	_____	car--	_____

l s sp pret		s th sl bl	
bend	_____	pink	_____
-end	_____	-ink	_____
-end	_____	--ink	_____
--end	_____	--ink	_____
----end	_____	--ink	_____

B Now choose the words to write under these pictures:

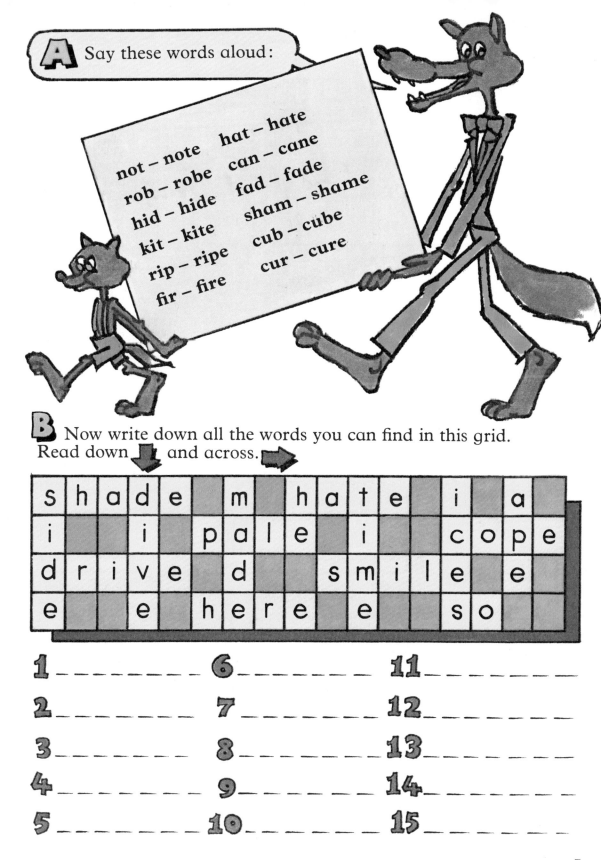

A Say these words aloud:

not – note   hat – hate
rob – robe   can – cane
hid – hide   fad – fade
kit – kite   sham – shame
rip – ripe   cub – cube
fir – fire   cur – cure

B Now write down all the words you can find in this grid.
Read down ⬇ and across. ➡

s	h	a	d	e		m		h	a	t	e		i		a	
i			i		p	a	l	e		i				c	o	p	e
d	r	i	v	e		d			s	m	i	l	e		e	
e			e		h	e	r	e			e			s	o	

1 _ _ _ _ _ _ _   6 _ _ _ _ _ _ _   11 _ _ _ _ _ _ _

2 _ _ _ _ _ _ _   7 _ _ _ _ _ _ _   12 _ _ _ _ _ _ _

3 _ _ _ _ _ _ _   8 _ _ _ _ _ _ _   13 _ _ _ _ _ _ _

4 _ _ _ _ _ _ _   9 _ _ _ _ _ _ _   14 _ _ _ _ _ _ _

5 _ _ _ _ _ _ _   10 _ _ _ _ _ _ _   15 _ _ _ _ _ _ _

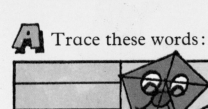

A Trace these words:

| lines | kites | nine | mice | five |

B Now put the right words under these pictures:

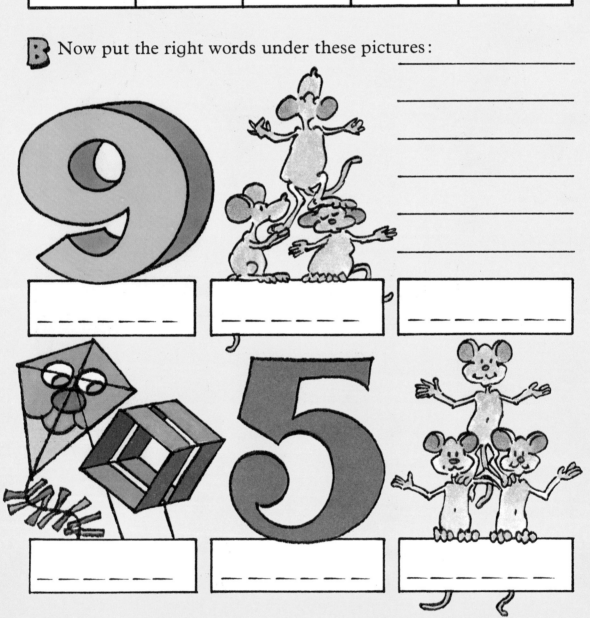

8

A Trace these words:

Diana | John | Liz | David | the sun

B Choose the missing word from the list.

1. Liz is going to _ _ _ _ _ _ _ _ _

2. Diana is going to _ _ _ _ _ _ _ _

3. The sun is going to _ _ _ _ _ _ _

4. John is going to _ _ _ _ _ _ _ _

5. David is going to _ _ _ _ _ _ _ _

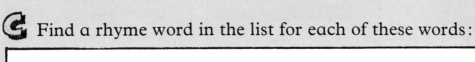

dive side
like mile
time rise
ride wife
mice wire
shine write

C Find a rhyme word in the list for each of these words:

1. tide _ _ _ _ _ _ _ _

2. line _ _ _ _ _ _ _ _

3. life _ _ _ _ _ _ _

4. kite _ _ _ _ _ _ _ _

5. crime _ _ _ _ _ _ _

6. fire _ _ _ _ _ _ _ _

7. five _ _ _ _ _ _ _ _

8. twice _ _ _ _ _ _ _

9. file _ _ _ _ _ _ _ _

10. wise _ _ _ _ _ _ _ _

Write the names under these pictures:

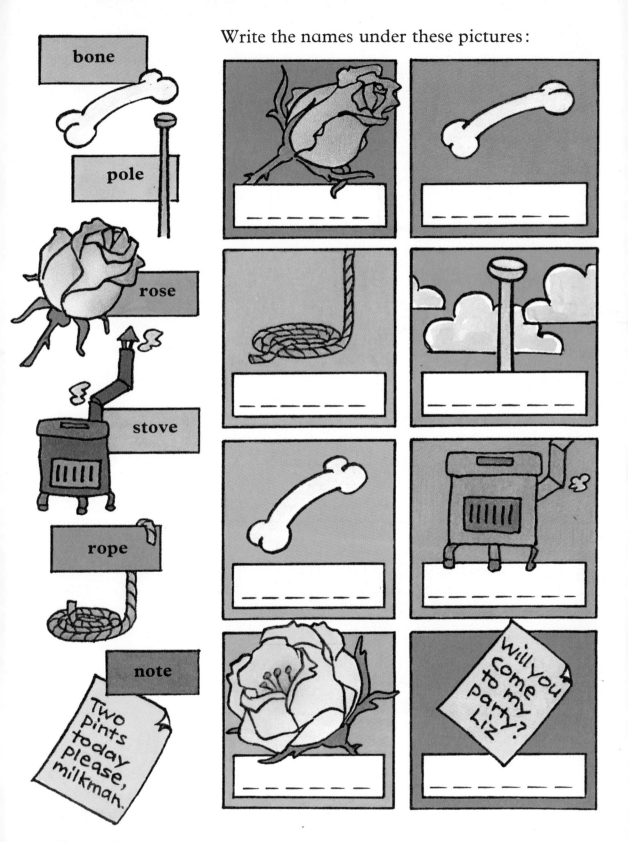

Trace these words:

| cake | names | face | plates | cage |

B Now choose the words to write under these pictures:

C Write the complete words, like this:

se me ve ge		ne ce te me	
cake	_cake_	lake	_____
ca--	_case_	la--	_____
ca--	_____	la--	_____
ca--	_____	la--	_____
ca--	_____	la--	_____

Choose the right word. Write it under the picture.

bite	
kite	
write	
spite	_ _ _ _ _ _

home	
stone	
rope	
hope	_ _ _ _ _ _

rake	
make	
cake	
bake	_ _ _ _ _ _

page	
face	
lake	
made	_ _ _ _ _ _

hose	
rose	
nose	
close	_ _ _ _ _ _

mole	
bone	
home	
code	_ _ _ _ _ _

time	
nine	
five	
twice	_ _ _ _ _ _

bikes	
tiles	
sides	
lines	_ _ _ _ _ _

What is it?
Do the puzzle
and find out.
Choose the words
from the list.

grapes   **wade**   **bike**   **smile**
white   **ice**   **bake**   **write**

1. You go through water when you do this.
2. You use a pen or pencil to do this.
3. You do this when you are happy.
4. You skate on this.
5. This is the colour of snow.
6. You do this in an oven.
7. You ride this.
8. You can eat these.

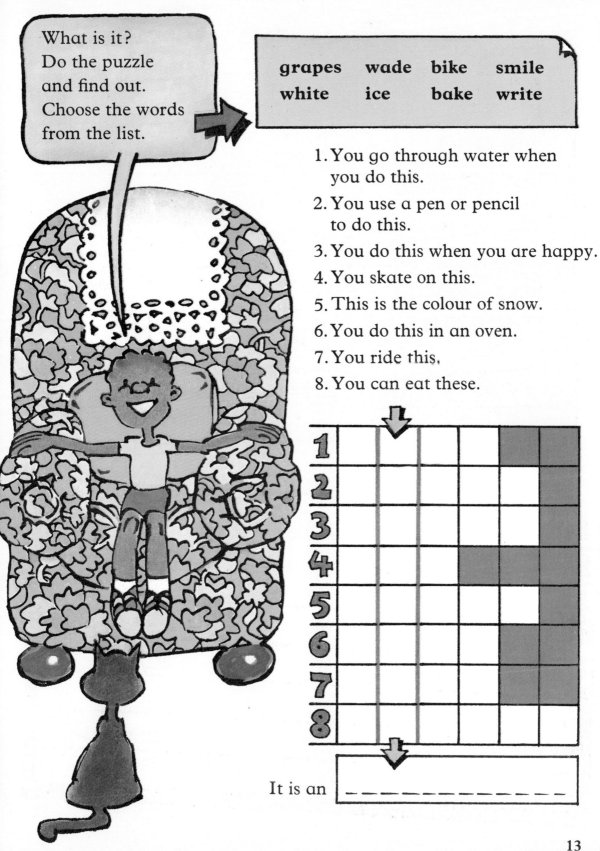

It is an _____

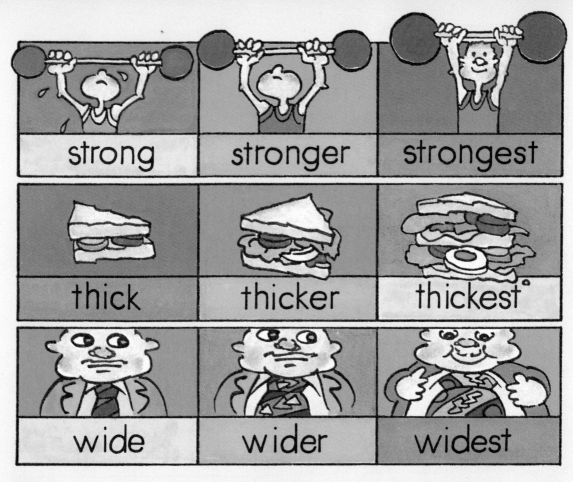

	strong	stronger	strongest
thick	thicker	thickest
wide	wider	widest

Now write the missing words here:

1	long	longer	
2	short		shortest
3	old		
4		nicer	
5			latest
6	poor		
7			smallest
8		younger	

14

Can you find the names of the things in this grid?
Write them under the pictures.

A Trace these words:

cliff   clock   clubs   cloak   cloud

B Find the words for the puzzle from the pictures.

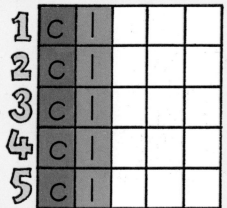

1	c	l		
2	c	l		
3	c	l		
4	c	l		
5	c	l		

1. It tells the time.

2. Rain drops from it.

3. You see them on cards.

4. It is a very steep hillside.

5. It is a coat that hangs loose.

C Write the complete words.

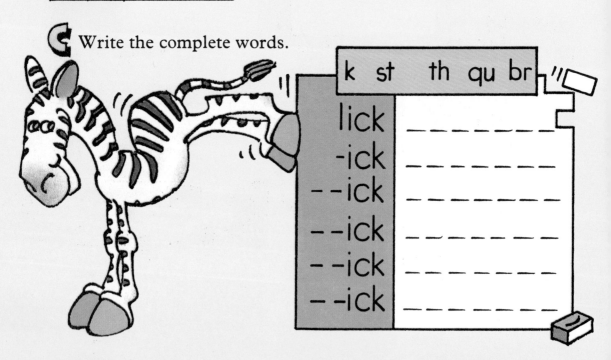

k st   th qu br

lick _____

-ick _____

--ick _____

--ick _____

--ick _____

--ick _____

A Trace these words:

| ear | beans | leaf | beak | east |

B Now choose the right words to put under these pictures:

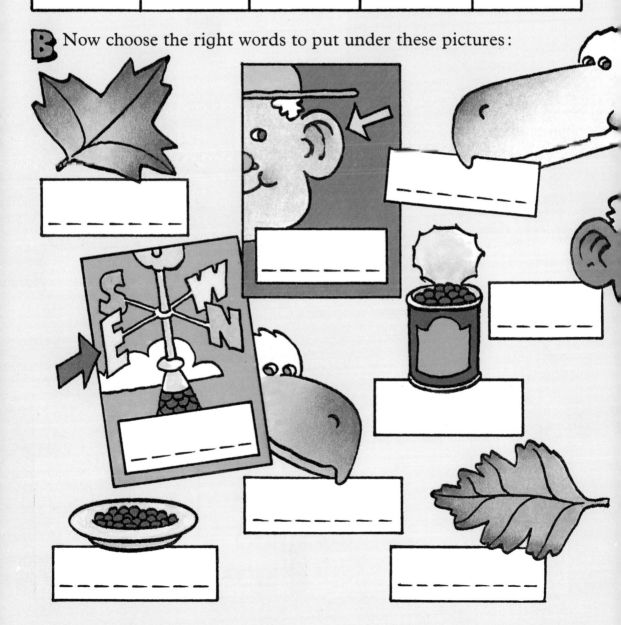

seat   beak
cheat   speak
cheap   beads
tea   year
team   clear
east   beard

A Choose the right word for each picture.

B Write the complete words.

m st rd ns	
beat	_____
bea-	_____
bea--	_____
bea--	_____
bea--	_____

p l r ve	
heat	_____
hea-	_____
hea-	_____
hea-	_____
hea--	_____

18

bite – biting	ride – riding	chase – chasing
dive – diving	drive – driving	write – writing
rake – raking	smile – smiling	make – making

A Choose the right –ing words for each picture, like this:

diving

_ _ _ _ _ _ _ _ _ _ _ _   _ _ _ _ _ _ _ _ _ _ _ _

_ _ _ _ _ _ _ _ _ _ _ _   _ _ _ _ _ _ _ _ _ _ _ _   _ _ _ _ _ _ _ _ _ _ _ _

  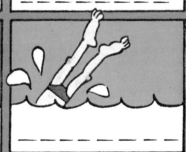

_ _ _ _ _ _ _ _ _ _ _ _   _ _ _ _ _ _ _ _ _ _ _ _   _ _ _ _ _ _ _ _ _ _ _ _

B Now make –ing words from these, like this:

1. save _ _ _ _ _ _ _ _ _ _ _   5. rule ruling

2. rise _ _ _ _ _ _ _ _ _ _   6. cure _ _ _ _ _ _ _ _ _

3. make _ _ _ _ _ _ _ _ _ _   7. vote _ _ _ _ _ _ _ _ _

4. joke _ _ _ _ _ _ _ _ _ _   8. wipe _ _ _ _ _ _ _ _ _

A Write out the complete words.

j cl dr str	
paw	_____
-aw	_____
--aw	_____
--aw	_____
---aw	_____

m bl gr beh	
kind	_____
-ind	_____
--ind	_____
--ind	_____
---ind	_____

h sl br str	
side	_____
-ide	_____
--ide	_____
--ide	_____
---ide	_____

m d tw sl	
rice	_____
-ice	_____
-ice	_____
--ice	_____
--ice	_____

B Choose the words to write under these pictures.

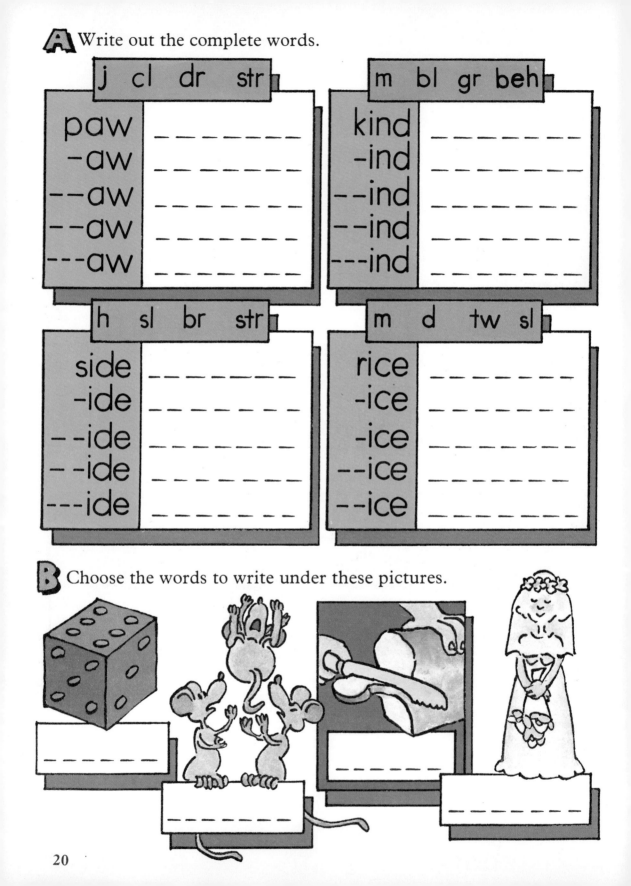

20

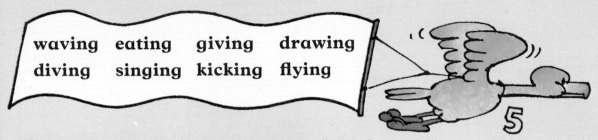

waving   eating   giving   drawing
diving   singing   kicking   flying

What is the baby in the bottom corner doing?
Fill in the puzzle and find out.

The baby is _ _ _ _ _ _ _ _ _ _ _

21

Write the complete words.

p f ch st	
hair	_ _ _ _ _ _
-air	_ _ _ _ _ _
-air	_ _ _ _ _ _
--air	_ _ _ _ _ _
--air	_ _ _ _ _ _

m sn sc bef	
bore	_ _ _ _ _ _
-ore	_ _ _ _ _ _
--ore	_ _ _ _ _ _
--ore	_ _ _ _ _ _
---ore	_ _ _ _ _ _

l bl dr pr	
mess	_ _ _ _ _ _
-ess	_ _ _ _ _ _
--ess	_ _ _ _ _ _
--ess	_ _ _ _ _ _
--ess	_ _ _ _ _ _

f r h gr	
sound	_ _ _ _ _
-ound	_ _ _ _ _
-ound	_ _ _ _ _
-ound	_ _ _ _ _
--ound	_ _ _ _ _

B Choose the right words to put under these pictures:

Arsenal 3
Luton 2

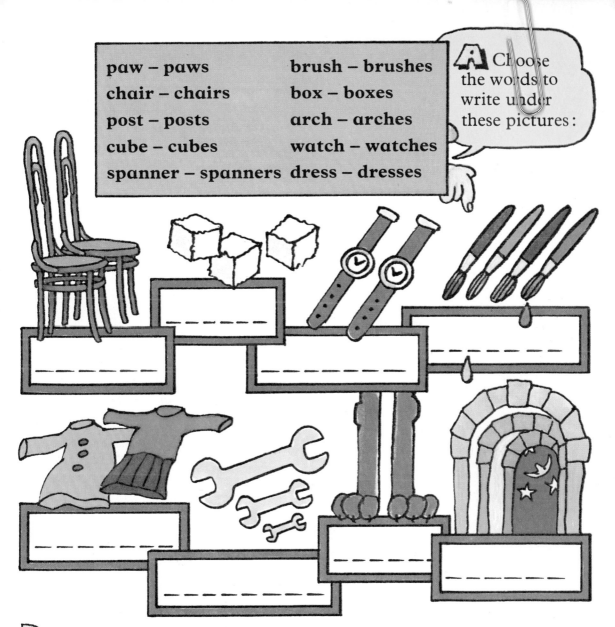

A Choose the words to write under these pictures:

paw – paws   brush – brushes
chair – chairs   box – boxes
post – posts   arch – arches
cube – cubes   watch – watches
spanner – spanners   dress – dresses

B To make a word mean more than one, you usually add –s (chair – chairs). But if the word ends in –sh, –x, –ch or –s, you add –es (brush – brushes).

Make these words mean more than one:

1. dish _ _ _ _ _ _ _   4. bush _ _ _ _ _ _   7. pair _ _ _ _ _ _ _

2. bunch _ _ _ _ _ _   5. fox _ _ _ _ _   8. kiss _ _ _ _ _ _ _

3. claw _ _ _ _ _ _ _   6. match _ _ _ _ _   9. stitch _ _ _ _ _ _ _

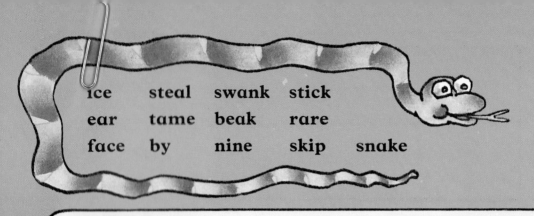

ice	steal	swank	stick
ear	tame	beak	rare
face	by	nine	skip	snake

What does the second row down say about the machine in the picture? Find out by doing the puzzle.

Find the rhyme for each word and write it in the puzzle.

1. fine
2. thick
3. rice
4. shame
5. cake
6. real
7. hear
8. trip
9. leak
10. care
11. drank
12. race
13. my